WORLD'S

FAVORITE

138 Easy To Play

MELODIES

For

ACCORDION

COMPILED
AND
EDITED BY
ALBERT GAMSE

ARRANGED BY
STEPHEN SECHAK

FOREWORD

The effectiveness and popularity of an earlier album (World's Favorite Series No. 8 — Easy to Play Accordion Pieces) has dictated the need for a supplementary publication of a similar nature, expanding the library and the choice of selections for the accordionist during the elementary period of his studies. 138 tunes have been selected to round out the repertoire of the beginner and to maintain and stimulate the interest of the mature player.

The notations in both volumes comply with the standard system approved by the American Accordionists' Association. For instance, chords for the left hand are in the bass clef. A dash under a bass note means that the note is played in the counter-bass. Bass solo notes are indicated: B.S. The small numbers above the chord roots designate:

1 — Major chord
2 — Minor chord
3 — Dominant 7th chord
4 — Diminished 7th chord

We have included a great variety of selections, including simple arrangements of esteemed classics and light concert pieces (without distorting the melodic appeal of the originals), blues, ragtime and popular tunes not available in any other current accordion collection, love songs of enduring quality, sacred music, famous marches and polkas, and simple folk songs.

It's the kind of book you will enjoy and appreciate more and more as the different segments unfold to enrich your musical career with a wealth of entertainment, education and technical proficiency.

The Publisher

DISTRIBUTED BY

HAL•LEONARD
CORPORATION

7777 W. BLUEMOUND RD. P.O. BOX 13819 MILWAUKEE, WI 53213

CLASSIFIED CONTENTS

CONTENTS

YOU'RE A GRAND OLD FLAG

GEORGE M. COHAN

AMERICA, THE BEAUTIFUL

SAMUEL A. WARD

DIXIE

D. D. EMMETT

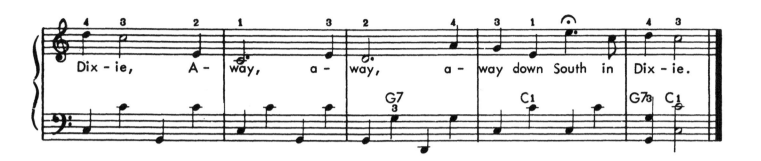

WHEN JOHNNY COMES MARCHING HOME

TRADITIONAL

AFTER THE BALL

CHARLES K. HARRIS

Af - ter the ball is o - ver, Af - ter the break of morn, ——— Af - ter the danc - ers leav – ing, Af - ter the stars are gone, ——— Man – y a heart is ach ——— ing, If you could read them all, ——— Man - y the hopes that have van ——— ished, Af - ter the ball.

MELODY OF LOVE

H. ENGELMANN

MY WILD IRISH ROSE

CHAUNCEY OLCOTT

MY GAL SAL

PAUL DRESSER

THE SIDEWALKS OF NEW YORK

(EAST SIDE, WEST SIDE)

LAWLOR-BLAKE

BEAUTIFUL BROWN EYES

Valse Moderato
VERSE: (girl)

TRADITIONAL

SWEET ROSIE O'GRADY

MAUDE NUGENT

IDA, SWEET AS APPLE CIDER

Lyric by
EDDIE LEONARD

Music by
EDDIE MUNSON

In The Shade Of The Old Apple Tree

Lyric by
HARRY WILLIAMS

Music by
EGBERT VAN ALSTYNE

HOME SWEET HOME

Lyric by
JOHN H. PAYNE

Music by
HENRY R. BISHOP

JAMAICA FAREWELL

TRADITIONAL

A DREAM

Text by
J. C. BARTLETT

Music by
CHARLES B. CORY

CLAIR DE LUNE

(DE LA SUITE BERGAMASQUE)

CLAUDE DEBUSSY

FASCINATION

F. D. MARCHETTI

GYPSY LOVE SONG

VICTOR HERBERT

LITTLE BROWN JUG

J. E. WINNER

MOSCOW NIGHTS

V. SOLOVIEV-SEDOY

THE FOGGY, FOGGY DEW

TRADITIONAL

AURA LEE

TRADITIONAL

2. Aura Lee, the bird may flee,
The willow's golden hair —
Swing through winter fitfully,
On the stormy air.
Yet if thy blue eyes I see,
Gloom will soon depart,
For to me, sweet Aura Lee,
Is sunshine through the heart.

3. In thy blush the rose was born,
Music when you spake,
Through thine azure eye the moon,
Sparkling, seemed to break.
Aura Lee, Aura Lee,
Birds of crimson wing,
Never song have sung to me,
As in that bright, sweet spring.

TOM DOOLEY

Moderato

TRADITIONAL

CHORUS:

2nd Verse: This time come to-morrow,
'Reckon where I'll be,
In some lonesome valley,
Hangin' from a tree.

(Repeat Chorus)

3rd Verse: Sittin' in this jail-house,
I'm in misery,
Had she not refused me,
Here I wouldn't be.

(Repeat Chorus)

ON TOP OF OLD SMOKY

TRADITIONAL

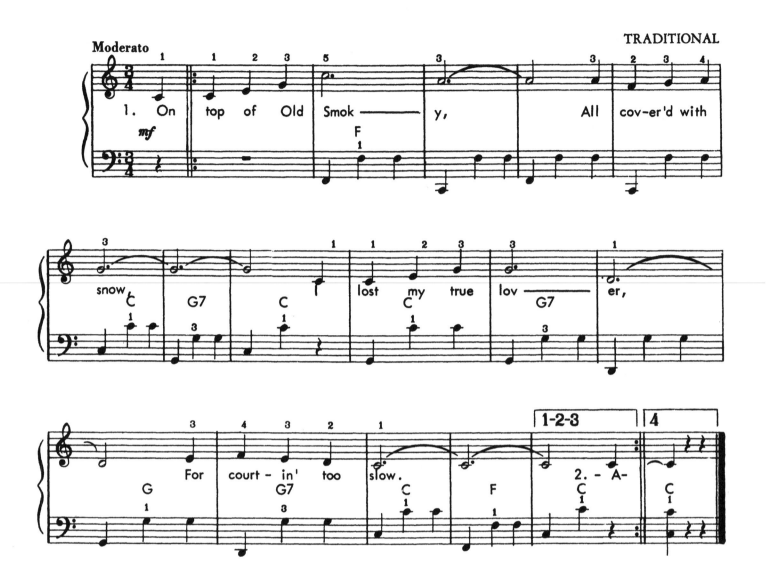

2. A-courtin's a pleasure,
    A-flirtin's a grief,
    A false-hearted lover —
    Is worse than a thief.

3. A thief, he will rob you,
    And take what you have,
    But a false-hearted lover —
    Sends you to your grave.

4. She'll hug you and kiss you,
    And tell you more lies —
    Than the ties on the railroad,
    Or the stars in the skies.

I GAVE MY LOVE A CHERRY

(THE RIDDLE SONG)

TRADITIONAL

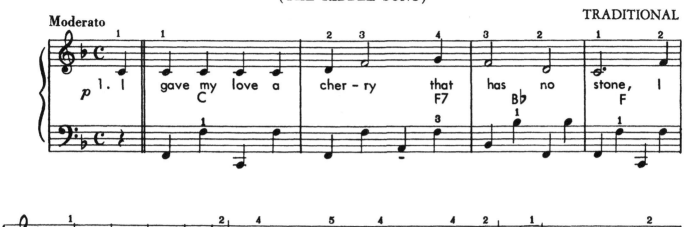

2. How can there be a cherry that has no stone?
How can there be a chicken that has no bone?
How can there be a ring that has no end?
How can there be a baby with no cry-en?

*(Instrumental to Fine)

3. A cherry when it's blooming, it has no stone,
A chicken when it's pipping, it has no bone,
A ring, when it's rolling, it has no end,
A baby, when it's sleeping, has no cryen.

*(Instrumental to Fine)

CARELESS LOVE

TRADITIONAL

THE BOWERY

Words by
C. HOYT

Music by
PERCY GAUNT

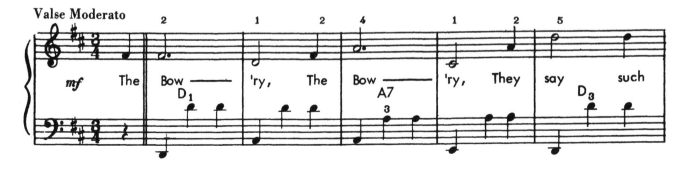

I WISH I WAS SINGLE AGAIN

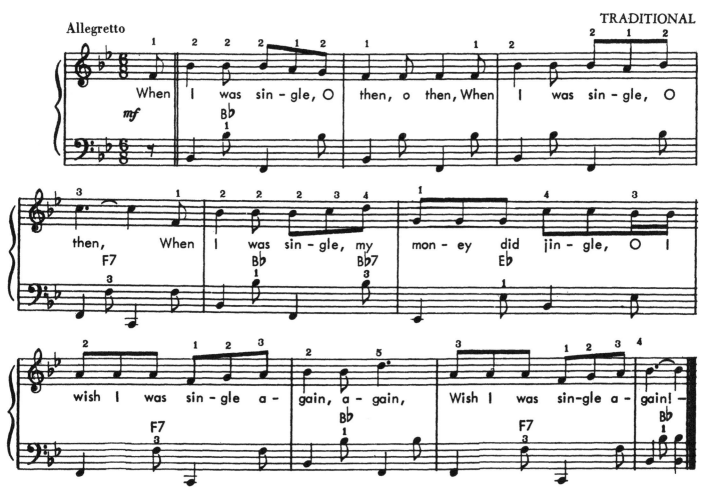

UNDER THE BAMBOO TREE

BOB COLE

The Man On The Flying Trapeze

TRADITIONAL

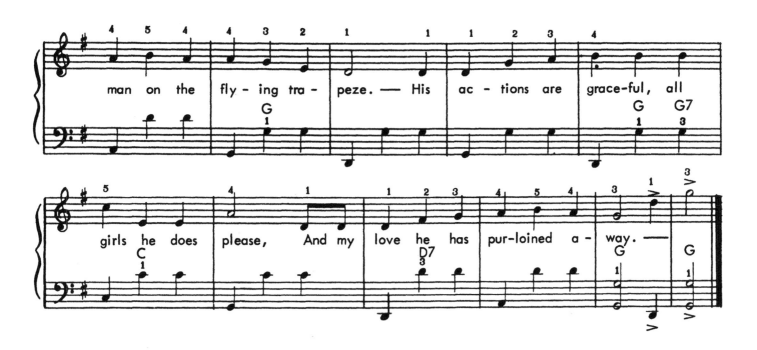

PAPER OF PINS

TRADITIONAL

Boy: I'll give to you a fine, silver spoon,
That you may feed your babes at noon,
If you will marry me, my love,
If you get married to me.

Girl: I won't accept the fine silver spoon,
That I may feed my babes at noon,
I will not marry you, not you,
I shan't be married to you.

Boy: I'll give to you my hand and my heart,
That we may wed and never part,
If you will marry me, my love,
If you get married to me.

Girl: If what you say is really sincere,
Then come into my arms, my dear,
And I will marry you, my love,
Yes, I'll get married to you.

THE BOLL WEEVIL SONG

TRADITIONAL

2.

Oh the first time I saw that little black bug,
He was settin' on the square,
The next time - that boll weevil -
Had a lot of his relations there,
Just a-lookin' for a home!
Just a-lookin' for a home!

3.

Oh the farmer, he went and took the boll,
And he put him in hot sand,
The weevil said - This hurts me,
But I'll tolerate it like a man,
'Cause I gotta have a home!
'Cause I gotta have a home!

4.

Oh the farmer, he told the merchant men,
We is in an awful fix,
The weevil et de cotton —
And he left us nothin' more than sticks,
And I'm gonna lose my home,
And I'm gonna lose my home!

FRANKIE AND JOHNNY

TRADITIONAL

2. Frankie was passing a hotel,
   Looked in a window so high,
   There she saw her lovin' Johnny,
   Making love to Alice Bly,
   He was her man, but he done her wrong.

3. Johnny saw Frankie a-comin',
   Down the back stairs he did scott,
   Frankie, she took out her pistal,
   And the gal could really shoot,
   He was her man, but he done her wrong.

4. Frankie was caught and arrested,
   She heard the judge calmly say:
   Lady, you're off to the jail house,
   They can throw the key away,
   He was a man, though he done you wrong.

5. Frankie, she said to the warden –
   What are they going to do?
   Warden replied, sorry Frankie,
   It's the 'lectric chair for you,
   You shot your man, and they say that's wrong.

6. Johnny was laid in his coffin,
   Rode in a carriage so black,
   Seven guys went to the graveyard,
   Only six of them came back,
   He was her man, but he done her wrong.

7. Frankie, she went to the big chair,
   Calm as a lady could be,
   Turning her eyes up, she whispered:
   Lord, I'm coming up to Thee,
   He was my man, but he done me wrong.

GIVE MY REGARDS TO BROADWAY

GEORGE M. COHAN

BILL BAILEY
(WON'T YOU PLEASE COME HOME?)

HUGHIE CANNON

DEAR OLD GIRL

Words by
RICHARD H. BUCK

Music by
THEODORE MORSE

Dear Old Girl, the rob - in sings a - bove you, Dear Old Girl, it speaks of how I love you, The blind-ing tears are fall - ing, As I think of my lost pearl, And my brok - en heart is call - ing, Call-ing for you, Dear Old Girl. ———

TA RA RA BOOM DER-E

HENRY J. SAYERS

Ta - ra - ra boom - di - ay, Ta - ra - ra boom - di - ay,
Ta - ra - ra boom - di - ay, Ta - ra - ra boom - di - ay!

A BIRD IN A GILDED CAGE

Lyric by
ARTHUR LAMB

Music by
HARRY VON TILZER

WHEN YOU WERE SWEET SIXTEEN

JAMES THORNTON

ON THE BANKS OF THE WABASH

PAUL DRESSER

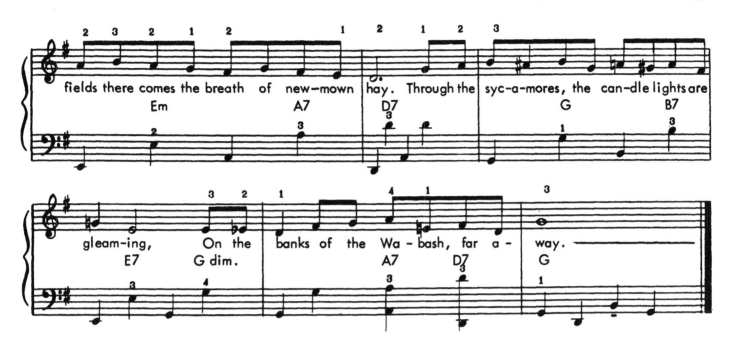

fields there comes the breath of new-mown hay. Through the syc-a-mores, the can-dle lights are

gleam-ing, On the banks of the Wa-bash, far a-way.

MICHAEL
(ROW THE BOAT ASHORE)

TRADITIONAL

Lento

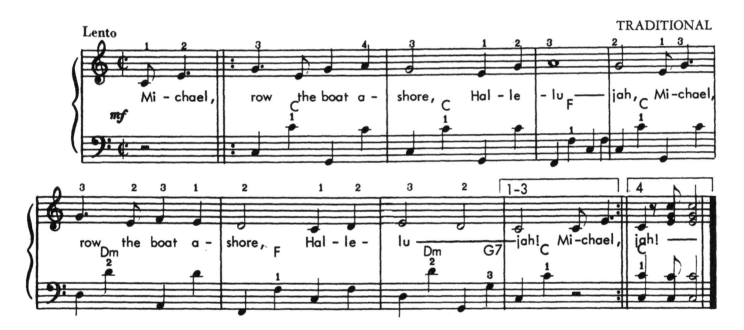

Mi - chael, row the boat a - shore, Hal - le - lu - jah, Mi-chael,

row the boat a - shore, Hal - le - lu - jah! Mi-chael, jah!

2. Sister, help to trim the sail,
Hallelujah,
Sister, help to trim the sail,
Hallelujah! (Repeat Michael &c)

3. Jordan River is chilly and cold,
Hallelujah,
Chills the body but not the soul,
Hallelujah! (Repeat Michael &c)

4. Jordan River is deep and wide,
Hallelujah,
Land of plenty on the other side,
Hallelujah! (Repeat Michael &c)

HELLO! MA BABY

Lyric by
JOSEPH E. HOWARD

Music by
IDA EMERSON

Brightly

MEET ME IN ST. LOUIS, LOUIS

Music by
KERRY MILLS
Moderato

Lyric by
ANDREW B. STERLING

IN THE GOOD OLD SUMMER TIME

GEORGE EVANS

Wait Till The Sun Shines, Nellie

Lyric by
ANDREW B. STERLING

Music by
HARRY VON TILZER

Moderato

ST. JAMES INFIRMARY

Andante Con Ritmo

TRADITIONAL

SIXTEEN TON

TRADITIONAL

Lyric by
AL GAMSE

MAPLE LEAF RAG

Music by
SCOTT JOPLIN

gal will throw him sweet and ten-der glanc-es, When he takes her danc-ing to the Maple Leaf Rag.

INSTRUMENTAL:

PARADE OF THE TIN SOLDIERS

Tempo di Marcia

LEON JESSEL

There Is A Tavern In The Town

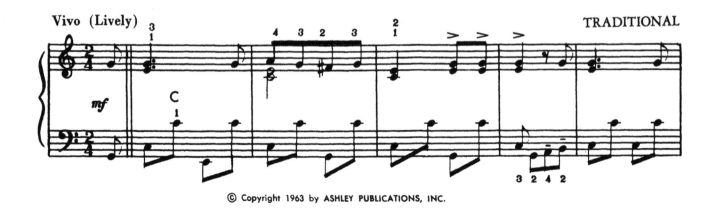

TRADITIONAL

THE WHISTLER'S POLKA

ROBERT VOGEL

HELENA POLKA

TRADITIONAL

BARNYARD POLKA

TRADITIONAL

Allegro vivo

DEEP RIVER

TRADITIONAL

SHORTNIN' BREAD

TRADITIONAL

SWING LOW, SWEET CHARIOT

Allegro Moderato

TRADITIONAL

NOBODY KNOWS THE TROUBLE I'VE SEEN

TRADITIONAL

LOVE'S OLD SWEET SONG

Words by
G. CLIFTON BINGHAM

Music by
J. L. MOLLOY

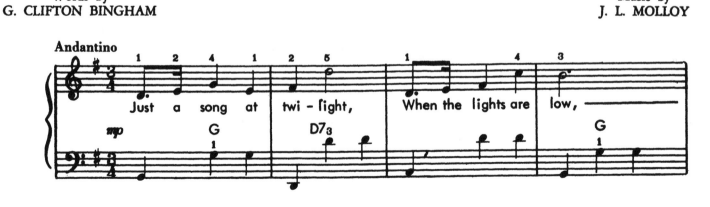

And the flick-'ring shad-ows — Soft-ly come and go. Tho' the heart be wea - ry,
Sad the day and long, —— Still to us at twi - light, ——
Comes love's old song, Comes love's old sweet song. ——

THE MEXICAN HAND-CLAPPING SONG
(CHIAPANECAS)

Lively

TRADITIONAL

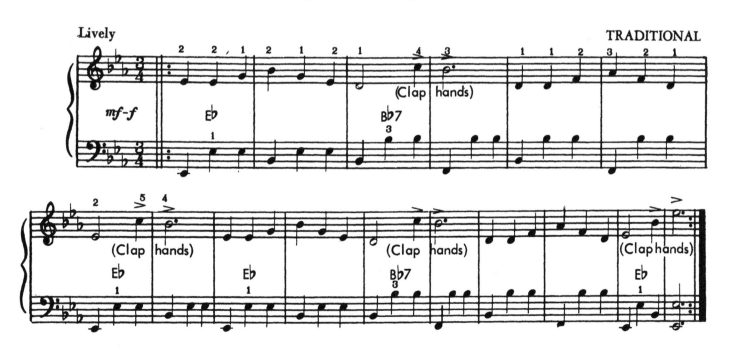

(Clap hands)

(Clap hands)

(Clap hands)

(Clap hands)

I'LL TAKE YOU HOME AGAIN, KATHLEEN

THOMAS P. WESTENDORF

64

I'll take you home a-gain, Kath-leen, A-cross the o-cean wild and wide, — To where your heart has ev-er been, Since first you were my bon-ny bride. The ros-es all have left your cheek, — I've watched them fade a-way and die, Your voice is sad when-e'er you speak, And tears be-dim your lov-ing eyes. Oh

REFRAIN

I will take you back, Kath-leen, To where your heart will feel no pain, And when the fields are fresh and green, — I'll take you to your home a-gain. —

THE SWEETEST STORY EVER TOLD

R. M. STULTS

TURKEY IN THE STRAW

TRADITIONAL

I LOVE YOU TRULY

CARRIE JACOBS-BOND

THE OLD KENTUCKY HOME

STEPHEN FOSTER

THE OLD FOLKS AT HOME

(SWANEE RIVER)

STEPHEN FOSTER

DANCE OF THE SLAVE MAIDENS

A. BORODIN

PRELUDE IN A

(OPUS 9, NO. 2)

FREDERIC CHOPIN

DON JUAN MINUET

Andante non troppo

WOLFGANG A. MOZART

AMARYLLIS

(AIR OF KING LOUIS XIII)

Moderato con moto

HENRI GHYS

73

SPRING, BEAUTIFUL SPRING

PAUL LINCKE

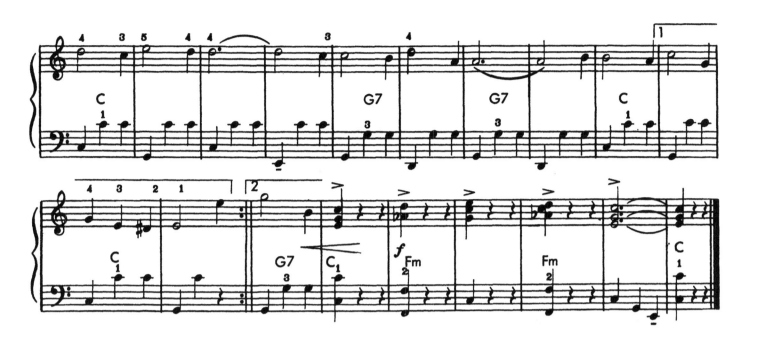

O SOLE MIO

(MY SUNSHINE)

Andante

E. DiCAPUA

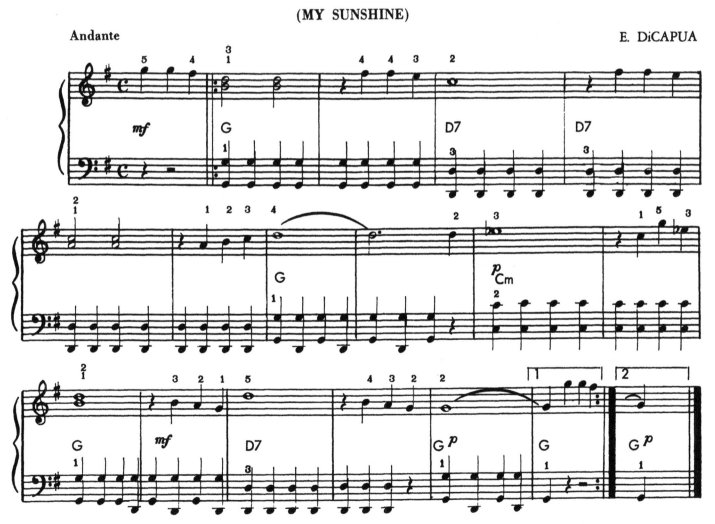

ELEGIE

JULES MASSENET

HUMORESQUE

ANTON DVORAK

NOCTURNE
(OPUS 9, NO. 2)

FREDERIC CHOPIN

SALUT D'AMOUR

(GREETING TO LOVE)

EDWARD ELGAR

SERENADE

FRANZ SCHUBERT

SURPRISE SYMPHONY

(THEME)

JOSEPH HAYDN

UNFINISHED SYMPHONY

FRANZ SCHUBERT

EMPEROR WALTZ

JOHANN STRAUSS

MINUET IN G

LUDWIG VAN BEETHOVEN

CONCERTO No. 1

Andante   **(THEME)**   PETER I. TSCHAIKOWSKY

ANDANTINO

EDWIN H. LEMARE

ETUDE No. 3

FREDERIC CHOPIN

THE PEARL FISHERS

GEORGES BIZET

AVE MARIA

BACH-GOUNOD

91

THE ROSARY

Words by
ROBERT CAMERON ROGERS
Lento

Music by
ETHELBERT NEVIN

WHAT CHILD IS THIS?

(GREENSLEEVES)

TRADITIONAL

SILENT NIGHT

Text by
JOSEPH MOHR

Music by
FRANZ GRUBER

STAR OF THE EAST

Lyric by
GEORGE COOPER
Moderato

Music by
AMANDA KENNEDY

DOLORES WALTZ

EMIL WALDTEUFEL

AH! SO PURE

(FROM "MARTHA")

FRIEDRICH VON FLOTOW

TOREADOR SONG

(FROM "CARMEN")

GEORGES BIZET

HAVAH NAGILAH
(LET US REJOICE)

TRADITIONAL

RAISINS AND ALMONDS

(ROJINKES MIT MANDLEN)

TRADITIONAL

Andante con moto

HATIKVOH

L. N. IMBER

WAVES OF THE DANUBE

(ANNIVERSARY WALTZ)

Moderato

JAN IVANOVICI

SAILOR'S HORNPIPE

TRADITIONAL

OVER THE WAVES

JUVENTINO ROSAS

CUCKOO WALTZ

J. E. JONASSON

LOVELIGHT TANGO

(A MEDIA LUZ)

EMILIO DONATO

BEAUTIFUL ISLE OF SOMEWHERE

Words by
JESSIE BROWN POUNDS

Music by
JOHN S. FEARIS

VALSE BLEUE

ALFRED MARGIS

RUSTIC DANCE

C. R. HOWELL

ADIOS MUCHACHOS
(FAREWELL, COMPANIONS)

J. SANDERS

LA CINQUANTAINE

(THE GOLDEN WEDDING)

GABRIEL-MARIE

JUANITA

Caroline Norton

IL BACIO
(THE KISS)

LUIGI ARDITI

SPRING SONG

FELIX MENDELSSOHN

MY HEART AT THY SWEET VOICE

(FROM "SAMSON AND DELILAH")

CAMILLE SAINT-SAENS

Moderato

CARNIVAL OF VENICE

G. LUDOVIC

FAUST WALTZ

CHARLES GOUNOD

MERRY WIDOW WALTZ

FRANZ LEHAR

WALTZ OF THE FLOWERS

(FROM "NUTCRACKER SUITE")

PETER I. TSCHAIKOWSKY

Moderato

O PROMISE ME

REGINALD DeKOVEN, Op. 50

Text by
EDWARD TESCHEMACHER

BECAUSE

Music by
GUY d'HARDELOT

WEDDING MARCH

(FROM "A MIDSUMMER NIGHT'S DREAM")

FELIX MENDELSSOHN

Allegro maestoso

BRIDAL CHORUS
(FROM "LOHENGRIN")

RICHARD WAGNER

Allegretto non troppo

FLOW GENTLY, SWEET AFTON

J. E. SPILLMAN

ANNIE LAURIE

WILLIAM DOUGLAS

LISTEN TO THE MOCKING BIRD

EDWARD HOFFMAN

mock-ing bird, Lis-ten to the mock-ing bird, Still sing-ing where the weeping wil-lows wave.—

SHE'LL BE COMIN' 'ROUND THE MOUNTAIN

TRADITIONAL

Allegro

1. She'll be com-in' 'round the mount-ain when she comes,———— She'll be

com - in' 'round the mount-ain when she comes.————— She'll be com-in' 'round the

mount-ain, She'll be com - in' 'round the mount-ain, She'll be com - in' 'round the

mount-ain when she comes.———

2. She'll be driving six white horses when
     she comes. (Repeat 4 times)
3. We will all go out to meet her when she
     comes. (Repeat 4 times)
4. She'll be huffin' and a-puffin' when she
     comes. (Repeat 4 times)
5. Repeat "She'll be comin' 'round — etc.

OH! THEM GOLDEN SLIPPERS

JAMES A. BLAND

THE OLD OAKEN BUCKET

Lyric by
SAMUEL WOODWORTH

Music by
C. KRALLMARK

DU DU LIEGST MIR IM HERZEN

(YOU'RE IN MY HEART)

TRADITIONAL

ACH! DU LIEBER AUGUSTIN
(OH! MY DARLING AUGUSTINE)

TRADITIONAL

THE EYES OF TEXAS

Words by
JOHN L. SINCLAIR
Vivo (Lively)

Music TRADITIONAL

Official Song of the University of Texas

RAMBLING WRECK

(FROM "GEORGIA TECH")

FRANK ROMAN

Official Song of the Georgia School of Technology

OUR DIRECTOR

F. E. BIGELOW

THE CAISSONS GO ROLLING ALONG

(FIELD ARTILLERY SONG)

TRADITIONAL

With spirit

POMP AND CIRCUMSTANCE

Marcato molto allegro

EDWARD ELGAR

UNDER THE DOUBLE EAGLE

J. F. WAGNER

TRIO

COLUMBIA, THE GEM OF THE OCEAN

With spirit

THOMAS BECKET

A FRANGESA

(TO FREEDOM)

P. MARIO COSTA

Molto allegro

ENTRY OF THE GLADIATORS

(THUNDER AND BLAZES)

JULIUS FUCIK

MEADOWLANDS

Slow March

TRADITIONAL

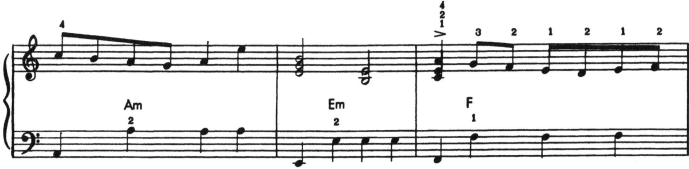

THE JOLLY COPPERSMITH MARCH

CARL PETER

D.S. al Fine

SEMPER FIDELIS
(FOREVER FAITHFUL)

JOHN PHILIP SOUSA

NATIONAL EMBLEM MARCH

E. E. BAGLEY

TRIO